*Opera*

Published by Smart Apple Media

1980 Lookout Drive, North Mankato, Minnesota 56003

Design and Production by EvansDay Design

Photographs: page 3: Leonard de Selva/CORBIS; page 7: James
L. Amos/CORBIS; pages 8, 23, 25: Bettmann/CORBIS; pages
10,11, 14: Archivo Iconografico, S.A./CORBIS; page 13: Adam
Woolfitt/CORBIS; page 17: Courtesy of Glyndebourne Festival
Opera; Ira Nowinski/CORBIS; pages 18, 22, 27, 31: Robbie
Jack/CORBIS; page 19: Richard Hamilton Smith/CORBIS;
page 21: Hulton-Deutsch Collection/CORBIS; page 28:
Michael S. Yamashita/CORBIS; page 29: Jacob Halaska

*Library of Congress Cataloging-in-Publication Data*

Gish, D. L.

Opera / by D. L. Gish

p. cm. — (World of music)

Includes index.

Summary: Provides history of the development of opera

music and discusses its styles and noted composers

and performers.

ISBN 1-58340-045-1

1. Opera—Juvenile literature. [1. Opera.] I. Title.

II. Series: World of music (North Mankato, Minn.)

ML1700.G52      2002

782.1—dc21      99-010872

First Edition

2  4  6  8  9  7  5  3  1

# OPERA

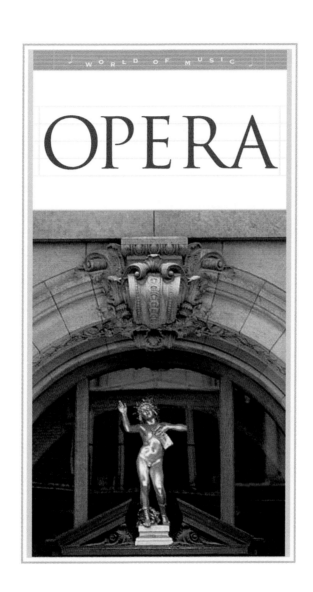

D. L. GISH

A STORM RAGES ACROSS A SMALL FISHING village. As people struggle to secure their boats, voices rise and fall with the wind. For Peter Grimes, the tempest frees him from his raging emotions. As the storm unleashes its fury on the village, so too does Peter unleash his guilt and anger. With his head lifted toward the dark skies, he raises his fists and screams at the top of his lungs. He screams for his apprentice, a young boy who drowned when he fell from Peter's fishing boat. To some people, opera may seem old-fashioned and even boring. But scenes such as this one, from *Peter Grimes*, composed by Benjamin Britten, show why this complex form of music and drama is still as unique and spellbinding today as it was more than four centuries ago.

# THE EARLIEST
# *Operas*

La Boheme *by Puccini is the most frequently produced opera. It is the story of a poor poet who falls in love with a seamstress dying of an incurable illness.*

OPERA'S BEGINNINGS CAN BE TRACED back to Florence, Italy, in 1597. A group of musicians and artisans, known as the Camerata, decided to experiment with the ancient Greek idea of combining music and drama to tell a story. This was the birth of opera.

The first operas were performed as oratorios, in which actors recited the words to a play in a simple singsong method, similar to children making up their own songs. No one actually followed any specific directions. Because of this, audiences soon became bored. Opera probably would have disappeared right then if it weren't for an Italian composer named Claudio Monteverdi.

Employed as a music director in Venice, Italy, Monteverdi established the various parts of modern opera. These included the instrumental overture, which gave audience members time to settle into their seats; the long vocal solo known as the aria; the large

FLORENCE, ITALY, THE BIRTHPLACE OF OPERA

group singing known as the chorus; and the interlude, which gave the stage hands time to change the scenery between acts. In 1607 Monteverdi's dramatic opera *Orfeo* was a huge success, and he went on to compose many more works.

HENRY PURCELL

*A lot of time and effort can go into creating sets for operas. As part of the set for the opera* The Rake's Progress *by Igor Stravinsky, a 1928 Model A car was rebuilt to look like a 1928 Mercedes.*

OPERA HAS ALWAYS BEEN IDENTIFIED with Italy because the Italian language works so well with the operatic form. But during the 17th and 18th centuries, opera made its way beyond Italy into the neighboring countries of France, Germany, and England. French opera began to flourish around 1672 when Jean Baptiste Lully (an Italian) composed one of France's first operas.

Reinhard Keiser is considered the true founder of German opera. He wrote more than 116 operas between 1694 and 1734. About this same time, Henry Purcell was composing operas in England. Lully, Keiser,

and Purcell helped establish a new kind of opera that was considered more grand and stately than Italian opera.

By this time, Italian opera had split into two different forms. *Opera seria* was based on tragic stories about noble historical figures. *Opera buffa* showed the funny side of ordinary citizens. These two forms of opera had gone their separate ways until Austrian Wolfgang Amadeus Mozart brought the two back together. While his great works, including *The Marriage of Figaro*, *Don Giovanni*,

and *The Magic Flute*, were created in the opera buffa form, they also included tragic elements. Mozart is considered the greatest opera composer of the late 18th century. He had an unusual talent for understanding and touching human emotions, and he expressed this talent through his music.

Scene from Mozart's *The Magic Flute*

*The first operas of the late 1600s and
early 1700s were considered simply
background music for card games, fancy
dinners, conversation, and fashion shows.*

IN THE EARLY 19TH CENTURY, OPERA
followed different paths in different countries. In Germany, composers turned toward more enchanting subjects. Operas were
created with stories in exotic settings. One
of Germany's greatest composers during this
time was the eccentric Richard Wagner.

Wagner created not only his own music,
but also his own plots, characters, text, and
scenery. He poured all of his emotions into
his work, which sometimes made him rather
unpopular with those around him. Wagner
will forever be remembered in the opera
world for his work *The Ring of the Nibelung,*

AUSTRIA'S VIENNA
STATE OPERA
THEATRE

GIOACCHINO ROSSINI

which took him nine years to complete. The four-opera epic totals 16 hours of performance time.

In Italy, composers were creating operas that showcased beautiful singing rather than instrumental music. This was called *bel canto opera*. Italy's greatest composer of the early 19th century was Gioacchino Rossini, who was a master at composing music for the voice. Rossini composed a string of 32 operas by the age of 30. His opera *William Tell* introduced the public to

*grand opera*, which uses serious and heroic stories, large choruses, and magnificent sets and costumes.

Another Italian composer who was greatly admired during the 19th century was Giuseppe Verdi, a man who grew up in poverty and was once turned down for a scholarship because of "insufficient talent." He based most of his works on the romantic authors of his time and filled his operas with intense drama. Unlike Richard Wagner, who stressed the opera's orchestration, Verdi felt that the quality of the singing was the most important feature.

# ACROSS
## the Ocean

*Italian-American composer Gian Carlo Menotti can claim two firsts in his career. His opera* The Old Maid and the Thief *(1939) was the first opera to be aired on radio. And his Christmas work,* Amahl and the Night Visitors *(1951), was the first opera to air on television.*

AROUND THIS SAME TIME, FRANCE WAS growing tired of grand, lavish operas and was eager for something different. Georges Bizet was one composer who met that need, creating operas that portrayed very serious real-life events.

In 1875 the world premiere of his opera *Carmen* was held at the Opera-Comique in Paris. *Carmen* is the story of an officer in the army who falls in love with a young gypsy girl. The opera created the feeling of impending disaster and built the suspense to the very end, which shocked audiences with its reality. Three months after the premiere of this

OPERA SINGER IN THE LEAD ROLE OF *CARMEN*

work, Bizet died, never knowing that one day *Carmen* would become one of the most popular musicals on the American Broadway stage.

While European countries had embraced opera in all its changing forms over the years, Americans didn't accept it right away. The first operas performed in the United States can be traced back to colonial days. Opera didn't become very popular, however. Most of the early colonists were Puritans who didn't believe in public displays of entertainment. Also, these immigrants

PERFORMERS IN THE OPERA *MADAM BUTTERFLY*

quickly scattered across a vast land. Home-
steading was hard work, which left little time
or money for such luxuries as opera.

Eventually, as Americans moved westward,
established new towns, and gained more
wealth, they started noticing what wealthy
Europeans were enjoying. Opera had always
been performed as a grand social event; it
was important for people to be seen there.
As this thinking was gradually adopted,
opera became entertainment for the
prosperous in the United States.

*Two composers who had many early failures were Giacomo Puccini and Giuseppe Verdi—now considered two of the most important composers in the history of opera.*

$B$Y THE EARLY 20TH CENTURY, BEAUTIFUL opera houses were being built in cities across the United States, allowing European composers to bring their works to a new audience. American composers began to have their share of success also. Virgil Thomson is considered one of America's first opera composers. Born in Missouri, Thomson studied in Paris and was influenced by many of the French composers. In his works, such as *Four Saints in Three Acts* (1928), he liked to use good humor and simple melodies.

Just as Thomson was influenced by the French, George Gershwin was influenced by

the popular American music of the time. In 1935 he created *Porgy and Bess,* the story of two lonely people in search of peace and happiness. This work is widely considered the most important of all American operas, blending jazz and serious music along with a grand stage show.

Another American composer who found much success in opera was Gian Carlo Menotti. He managed to master two very different types of works: *The Medium* (1946) was dramatic, while *The Telephone* (1947) was a lighthearted spoof. One of the few operas

*Italian Alessandro Scarlatti, who died in 1725, wrote an amazing 115 operas. Unfortunately, most of his work has been lost over time.*

written by an African-American is *Treemon-isha*, which was created by Scott Joplin, best known for his turn-of-the-century ragtime music. Joplin also created *The Maple Leaf Rag*. Though *The Maple Leaf Rag* was finished by 1897, this ragtime opera did not make its professional premiere until 1975.

SCENE FROM
*PORGY AND BESS*

# ROCK
## *Opera*

*In 1999, the Santa Fe Opera installed small screens on the back of every seat so that audience members could read along with the opera. The cost of this electronic system was two million dollars.*

A CONTEMPORARY FORM OF OPERA IS the ballad opera, sometimes called rock opera. This form combines popular music with up-to-date sets and costumes, making it more attractive to a new and younger audience. Two well-known ballad operas are *Joseph and the Amazing Technicolor Dreamcoat* and *Jesus Christ Superstar*; both were composed by Andrew Lloyd Webber, together with lyricist Tim Rice. Every year, these operas are staged in cities all over North America, from college theaters to major venues. Rock star Pete Townsend of The Who created the rock opera *Tommy* in 1969. Film versions of many

contemporary operas are also produced. In addition, soundtrack recordings are usually released around the same time that the operas open on stage or on film.

Movies that have nothing to do with opera may also include opera music in their soundtracks. The films *Jumanji* and *Mrs. Doubtfire* use music from Rossini's opera *The Barber of Seville*. The King Arthur epic, *Excalibur*, uses Wagner's *The Ring of the Nibelung* as its entire film score. Some movies even include opera as an element of the story, including *Moonstruck, Pretty Woman, The Mighty Ducks,* and *Foul Play.*

# *Stars*

*Jenny Lind (1820–1887), known as "the Swedish nightingale," was the most famous singer of her time. She drew crowds at every major opera house in Europe, then toured the U.S. with P.T. Barnum before moving to England in 1852.*

OPERAS ARE TECHNICAL UNDERTAKINGS that require a lot of time, money, and talent. One of the greatest expenses of opera is the cost of performers. Opera singers are a unique group. To become an opera singer usually takes years of training. While there have been many wonderful male and female opera singers over the years, today the most well-known are probably Luciano Pavoratti, Placido Domingo, and Jose Carreras—The Three Tenors.

Because of the mounting costs of staging a performance, many opera companies feel it's too risky to put on productions of new com-

COSTUMED
PERFORMERS IN A
CHINESE OPERA

posers. Often opera houses will have a sele-ction of operas that they run throughout a season. This is called a repertoire, and it helps to keep costs down because the same performers, costumes, stage settings, and musicians can be used continually. This makes it hard for new composers to get their works produced. Furthermore, many opera fans are loyal to the classics and prefer to see the works of such famous composers as Mozart, Verdi, Rossini, and Wagner.

Today, operas are staged in hundreds of elegant opera houses in countries all around the world. Famous opera houses are as valued as the stars who sing inside them. Some of the most important opera houses in the world include the Metropolitan Opera House in New York, La Scala in Italy, the Paris Opera House in France, and the Sydney Opera House in Australia.

*Many Chinese operas include acrobatics and martial arts in their performances. The instruments used for the music include bowed and plucked lutes, gongs, clappers, drums, reeds, and flutes.*

Billy Budd *by Benjamin Britten is an opera consisting of male performers only. On the other hand, Puccini's* Suor Angelica, *which takes place in a convent, was created for an all-female cast.*

MANY OPERA COMPANIES TODAY ARE trying to find a happy balance between the old and the new. They continue to stage the classic works while still allowing new composers to experiment with the stage. Some of the more unusual productions in the last two or three decades include two politics-related operas by American composer John Adams and an adaptation of the Tennessee Williams play *A Streetcar Named Desire* by Andre Previn. Recently, the Metropolitan Opera House hired composer John Harbison to create an opera based on F. Scott Fitzgerald's 1925 novel, *The Great Gatsby.*

Other modern productions are related to popular movies, such as Disney's *The Lion King* and *Beauty and the Beast*. These kinds of operas differ from rock operas in that the stories are geared toward children. This in itself is a new—and very popular—concept for opera. The Disney productions consistently fill theaters with parents and children. New storylines, experimental music, and exciting new sound and light technology have helped to bring this centuries-old musical form into the 21st century.

**A**
Adams, John 30

**B**
Bing, Sir Rudolf 11
Bizet, Georges 16, 18
Britten, Benjamin 5, 30

**C**
Caldwell, Sarah 15
(the) Camerata 6

**D**
Domingo, Placido 26, 27

**G**
Gershwin, George 20–22

**H**
Harbison, John 30

**J**
Joplin, Scott 23

**K**
Keiser, Reinhard 9–10
Kennedy Center Award for
Excellence 15

**L**
Lind, Jenny 26
Lully, Jean Baptiste 9

**M**
Menotti, Gian Carlo 16, 22
Monteverdi, Claudio 7
movies 25, 31
Mozart, Wolfgang Amadeus 10–11, 28

**O**
Opera
American 18–19, 20, 22–23, 30
ballad/rock 24-25, 31

bel canto 14
Chinese 28, 29
companies 30–31
English 9–10
French 9, 16–18, 20
German 9, 12–14
houses 11, 13, 19, 24, 28, 29, 30
Italian 6–8, 9, 14–15, 23
origins of 6–8
parts of 7–8
Opera-Comique 16
oratorios 6

**P**
Previn, Andre 30
Puccini, Giacomo 6, 20, 21, 30
Purcell, Henry 8, 9–10

**R**
Rice, Tim 24
(The) Ring of the Nibelung 14, 25
Rossini, Gioacchino 14–15, 25, 28

**S**
Scarlatti, Alessandro 23
Stravinsky, Igor 9

**T**
television 11, 16
Thomson, Virgil 20
(The) Three Tenors 26
Townsend, Pete 24

**V**
Verdi, Giuseppe 15, 20, 28

**W**
Wagner, Richard 12–15, 25, 28
Webber, Andrew Lloyd 24